W9-BYD-003

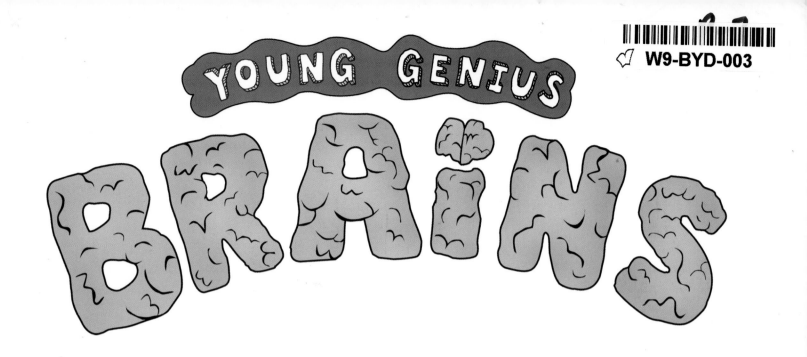

YOUNG GENIUS

BRAINS

For Zoom Rockman — K. L.
To Mum and Dad — E. G.

First edition for the United States, its dependencies,
the Philippines, and Canada published in 2007
by Barron's Educational Series, Inc.

First published in 2006 in Great Britain by
Hutchinson, an imprint of
Random House Children's Books

All inquiries should be addressed to:
Barron's Educational Series, Inc.
250 Wireless Boulevard
Hauppauge, New York 11788
www.barronseduc.com

Library of Congress Control Number: 2006932168

ISBN-13: 978-0-7641-3670-2
ISBN-10: 0-7641-3670-4

Printed in China
9 8 7 6 5 4 3 2 1

Inside your head,
behind your eyes,
is an amazing machine
called your **brain.**

Your brain
has a wiggly,
wrinkled surface.

If you were to iron out all the wrinkles,
there would be enough material to make this
alien outfit . . .

CooL!

If you could touch your brain,
it would feel wet and wobbly,
like a **big pink Jello mold**.

Jello can squash really easily . . .

But you have a strong case
made of bone
to keep your brain safe.
It's called your
skull.

goo

skull

brain

Your skull is full of **goo**
so that your brain
can move about
without banging
into the sides!

Imagine that your head
is this boiled egg.

If you were to
take off the top,
you would see your brain.
It would look like this.

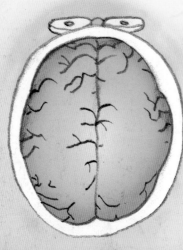

Your brain is made up of
two halves.

The
left half
works
everything
on the
right side
of your
body.

It is possible to look at your brain without taking it out of your head.

A big machine can take a photograph called a **scan**.

Scans can be taken at spaces across the head, like slices through a loaf of bread.

Here is another view of the brain, this time from the side.

The long piece at the bottom is called the **brainstem.**

It's a bit like the stem of a flower.

The brainstem pokes down through your neck. Its job is to carry the right amount of blood and air up to your brain.

If your brain doesn't get enough blood and air, it will start to hurt.

This is called a **headache**.

You can get a headache if you sleep with your neck in a funny position like this.

Every creature has a brain:

fish

elephants

monkeys

giraffes

squirrels

even this tiny flea!

Animals with bigger brains aren't always smarter than those with smaller ones.

This clever bee knows how to make delicious honey.

But this silly cow is standing in her own poo **again!**

Humans are very clever.
But other animals are clever, too,
like these smart little
dolphins.

They can understand
sign language
and do fantastic tricks.

And they can answer
simple questions like,
Do you want a fish?

or,
*Do you want a bucket
on your head?*

Dolphins speak to each other by making funny whistling and clicking noises. Unfortunately, nobody knows what they're talking about. So it's hard to find out *just* how clever they are.

We do know that a dolphin can find its way around underwater – even in the darkest places at the bottom of the ocean – like a **submarine**. Now that is **clever!**

A baby's brain is as heavy as an **apple**.

My brain is as heavy as a **potato**.

A teacher's brain is as heavy as a **pumpkin**.

And a bird's brain is as heavy as half a **pea**!

You use your brain
when you need
to remember something,
like your address
or what you had for breakfast.

Your brain stores
the memory
deep inside.
This is called
learning.

If you are trying to learn something new, like the name of this planet, try saying it over and over again, closing your eyes and seeing it as a picture.

SATURN

BUZZzzzzz

SATURN is yellow with amazing striped rings, so imagine that you "sat on" a bumble bee.

That should help the memory to stick!

You need to go to sleep at night
so that your brain
can deal with everything you
have done during the day.

It plays with all the memories
by making up jumbled stories
and telling them as **dreams**.

**Can you remember
what you dreamed about
last night?**

Zzzzzzz

Bad dreams are called
nightmares.
Lots of people have them.
But they disappear
when you wake up.

The more you learn,
the quicker your brain will be
at remembering things,
and coming up with answers
to puzzles like these . . .

How many more words
can you make out of the letters
B R A I N?

rain   ban   an   nib

Which brain
is the same as this one?

Which brain
belongs to which body?

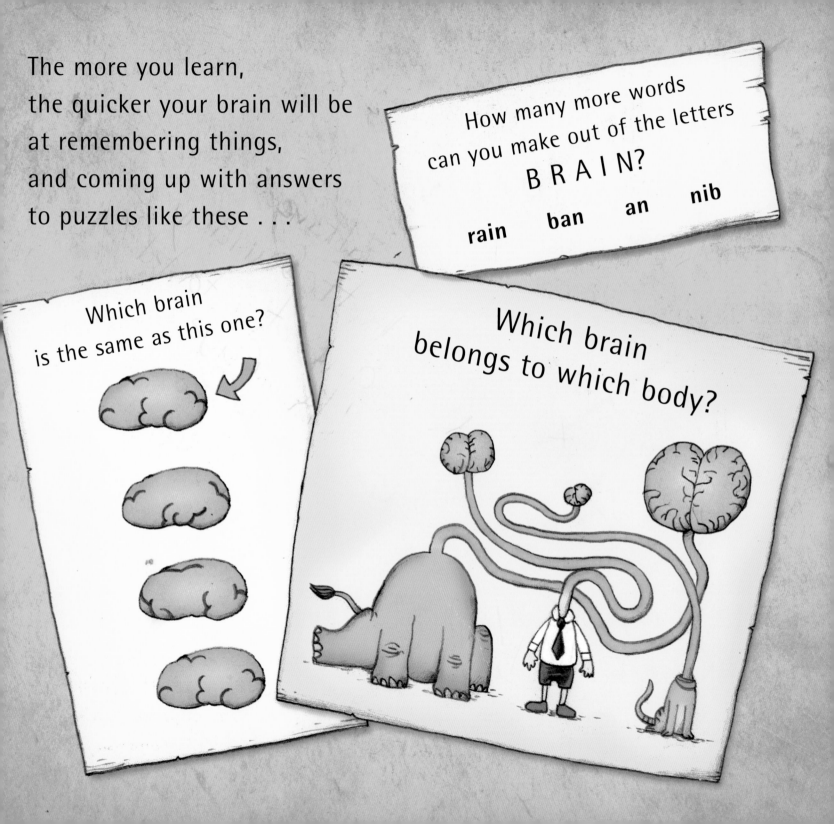

Sometimes you can picture things in your head that nobody has ever seen before. This is called **imagination**.

Looking

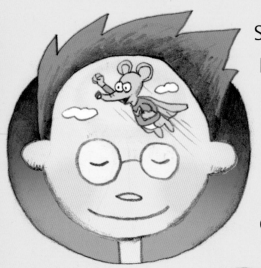

Some people can't do puzzles but have brilliant imaginations.

They can think up ideas and tell them as drawings and paintings, or write them as stories.

Yum!

Tasting

Reading is very good for your imagination. New words and ideas help your brain grow strong and clever.

Listening

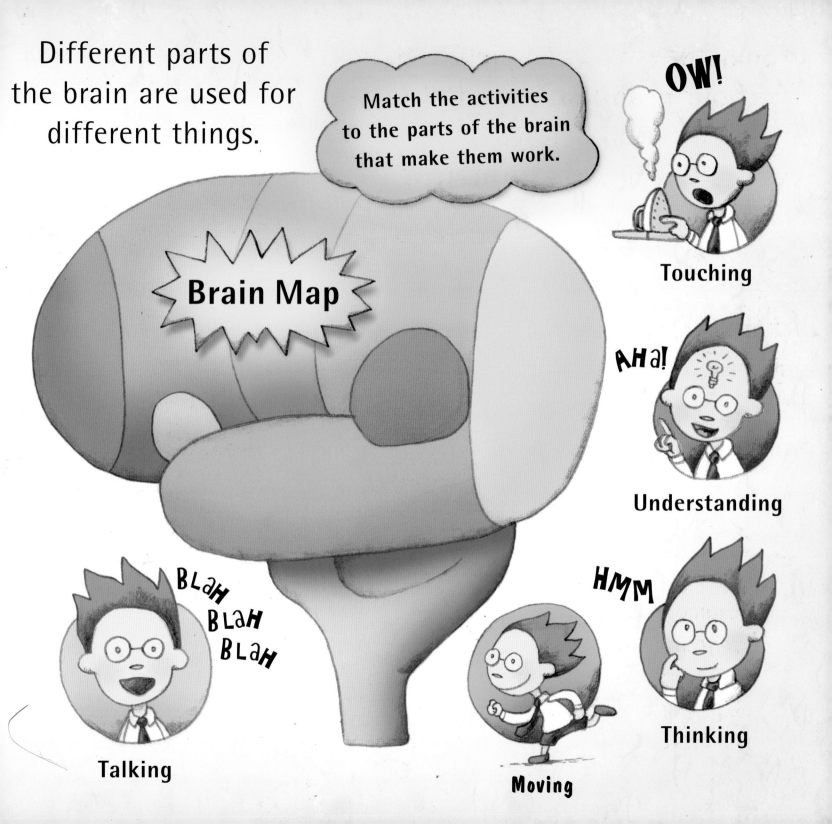

Bad brain juice comes from:

smoking

being told off too much

greasy food

too much TV

or playing on the computer

late nights

spending too much time on your own

This man is not looking after his brain.

The horrible mix of brain juice is tricking him into thinking he needs more bad stuff to stay happy.

A damaged brain can't mend itself like a cut finger.

Some people wear special hats to protect their brains when they are working.

firefighters

police officers

builders

And when they are having fun.

skaters

cyclists

If you ride a bike, don't forget to wear a **helmet**.

You don't want to end up with a brain like **scrambled eggs!**

I'm going to really look after my brain.

I don't just use it to say clever things.
I use it to think of funny riddles too, like,

How do two brains say good-bye?

With a **BRAIN WAVE!**

Good-bye!

That was everything I found out about **brains**.

This man knows a lot about brains. He's a **brain surgeon**.

A brain surgeon is a special type of doctor who mends people's brains if they aren't working properly.

To be a brain surgeon you need to have lots of good brain juice.

I'd like to be
a brain surgeon
when I grow up.

Would you?